W9-BRJ-527

Watch It Grow

Bean

Barrie Watts

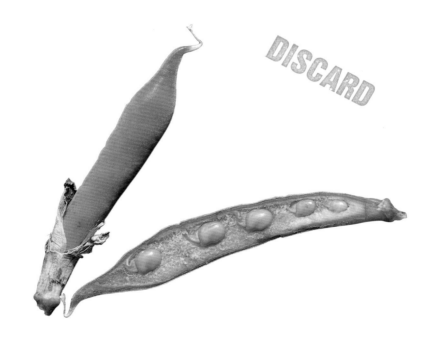

DISCARD

Smart Apple Media

First published in 2004 by Franklin Watts
96 Leonard Street, London EC2A 4XD, United Kingdom
Franklin Watts Australia, 45-51 Huntley Street, Alexandria, NSW 2015
Copyright © 2004 Barrie Watts

Editor: Kate Newport, Art director: Jonathan Hair,
Photographer: Barrie Watts, Illustrator: David Burroughs

Published in the United States by Smart Apple Media
2140 Howard Drive West, North Mankato, Minnesota 56003

U.S. publication copyright © 2005 Smart Apple Media
International copyright reserved in all countries. No part of this book may
be reproduced in any form without written permission from the publisher.
Printed in Hong Kong

Library of Congress Control Number: 2004101772

ISBN 1-58340-503-8

2 4 6 8 9 7 5 3 1

How to use this book

Watch It Grow has been specially designed to cater to a range of reading and learning abilities. Initially children may just follow the pictures. Ask them to describe in their own words what they see. Other children will enjoy reading the single sentence in large type in conjunction with the pictures. This single sentence is then expanded in the main text. More adept readers will be able to follow the text and pictures by themselves through to the conclusion of the bean's life cycle.

Contents

Beans come from seeds.

This bean seed is about half an inch (1.5 cm) long. A new bean plant will grow from it. It has a hard, tough skin that protects the inside parts of the seed from drying out.

Inside the seed is a store of food. Bean seeds are kept in a cool, dry place during the winter until they are ready to be planted.

The bean is planted.

The seed is planted when the weather becomes warmer in the spring. The seed needs warmth and water to start to grow.

As soon as the seed is planted, the moist soil starts to soften the skin. Water reaches the inside of the seed, and it starts to swell. The seed skin then splits.

The bean sprouts.

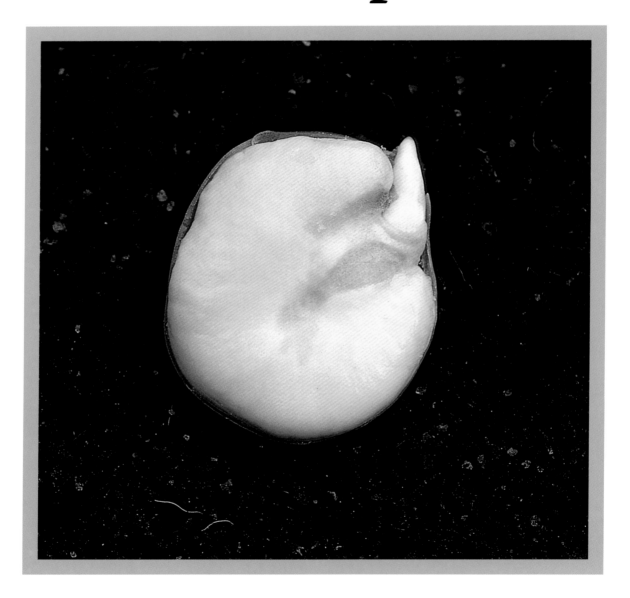

As the skin softens and splits,
the seed is able to grow a tiny
root from its top.

At first the root grows upward, but soon it turns around and grows down into the soil. It begins to take in **moisture** and **nutrients** from the soil.

The seed leaves start to grow.

After a week, a pair of leaves called **seed leaves** emerge from the seed and grow toward the surface of the soil.

They are folded downward so they do not get damaged as they push through the soil. **Moisture** collected by the new roots helps the leaves grow.

The seed leaves push upward.

The seed leaves grow on a stem that pushes them through the soil. When they reach the surface, the leaves begin to open up.

As it grows, the plant uses up the supply of food stored in the seed. When it is full-grown, it will make its own food.

Larger leaves grow.

The **seed leaves** absorb sunlight and—with the water from the roots— make food for the plant. This is called **photosynthesis**.

With this extra food, the plant can grow a stem and larger leaves. The large leaves have thin tubes in them called **veins**. Food is passed around the plant through the veins.

The roots grow.

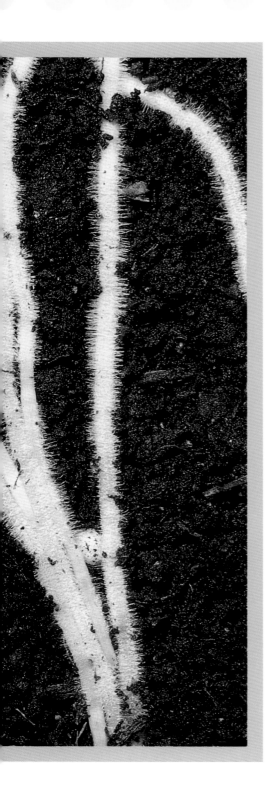

By now, the bean plant has grown many more roots in the soil. Tiny hairs on the roots take in more **moisture** and **nutrients** from the soil. The more nutrients the seed gets, the quicker it will grow. The network of roots also anchors the plant into the ground, enabling it to grow tall and strong.

The stem is strong.

The bean plant's stem grows upward and is thin and strong. It is hollow and made from tough, **flexible** fibers. It has to be strong because it must support all of the plant's leaves, flowers, and seeds without breaking.

Just below the stem's green skin are **veins** that carry water and food between the leaves and the roots.

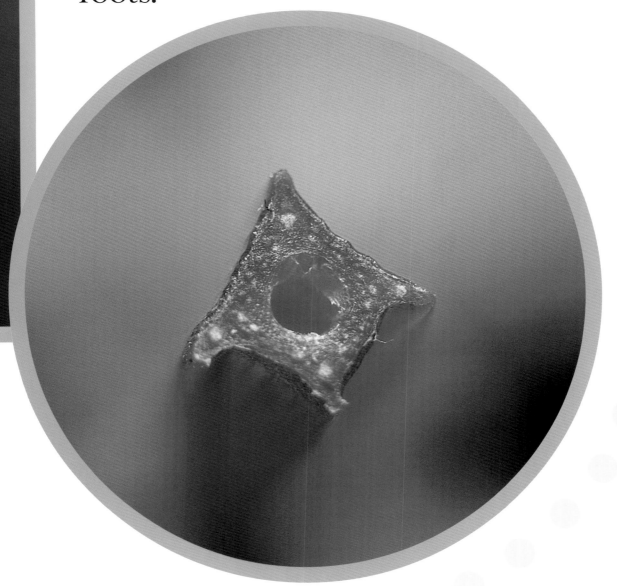

The flowers grow.

About two weeks after being planted, the plant begins to grow flower buds. They grow at the top of the plant on their own thin stems. As the stem gets taller, the plant continues to grow flower buds. The first flowers open up about 10 days after appearing as buds.

Bees visit the flowers.

When the flowers open, they make **nectar** and **pollen**. The flowers give off a strong scent to attract bees and other insects. Bees then visit the flowers in search of food.

To get to the nectar, bees have to brush past the **stamen** that holds the pollen. They then carry the pollen to the **stigma** of another flower and pollinate it.

The flower dies.

After pollination, the flowers die.
The petals start to wither and fall
off. The plant is now five weeks old
and begins to grow seedpods.

There are usually between 6 and 10 seedpods on a bean plant. The flowers that are not pollinated will die without growing into a seedpod.

The seedpod grows.

The seedpod gets bigger. Inside
the pod are the seeds. They grow
by taking food from the bean
plant, using the **veins** in the stem.

The young seeds are easily damaged by insects and need to be protected. The inside of the pod is soft and fuzzy. The outer skin is tough to keep the seeds from drying out.

The plant dies.

About 12 weeks after planting, the seedpods reach their full size: about eight inches (20 cm) long. The bean plant then dies. Many seedpods are harvested for people to eat.

Other seeds are kept and planted the following spring to grow new bean plants. If the pods are not harvested, they split and fall to the ground to grow into new plants.

Word bank

Flexible - easy to bend, like a piece of wire.

Moisture - when something is wet, like soil, it is said to have a lot of moisture in it.

Nectar - a sweet, sugary liquid that attracts bees and other insects to flowers. Bees make honey from nectar.

Nutrients - substances in soil that help plants grow.

Photosynthesis - the process by which leaves make food for a plant by absorbing sunlight and taking in water from their roots.

Pollen - a fine powder made by the male parts of a flower. It fertilizes the female parts to help a plant make new seeds.

Seed leaves - the first leaves that grow on a plant. When larger leaves start to grow, seed leaves die.

Stamen - the male part of the flower that produces pollen.

Stigma - the female part of a flower that makes nectar. When a stigma is fertilized by pollen, a seed starts to grow.

Veins - the tiny tubes in a leaf or stem that carry food and water around the plant.

Life cycle

Soon after planting, the
seed skin splits and
grows a root.

Twelve weeks after planting,
the seedpods reach their full
size and the plant dies.

After a week, a
pair of seed leaves
emerge and grow
toward the surface
of the soil.

The seedpod gets
bigger. Inside the pod
are the seeds.

The seed leaves grow on
a stem that pushes them
through the soil.

After pollination, the flowers
die. Five weeks after planting,
the plant grows seedpods.

After two weeks, the
plant begins to grow
flower buds. The
flowers make nectar.

The nectar attracts
insects that carry the
pollen to other flowers
and pollinate them.

Index